Scale Studies for the Third Octave for the Cello, Book One, by Cassia Harvey

CHP165

©2011 by C. Harvey Publications All Rights Reserved.

www.charveypublications.com - print books
www.learnstrings.com - PDF downloadable books
www.harveystringarrangements.com - chamber music

Scale Studies for the Third Octave

1

Cassia Harvey

Note: The scales studied in this book are listed at the end.

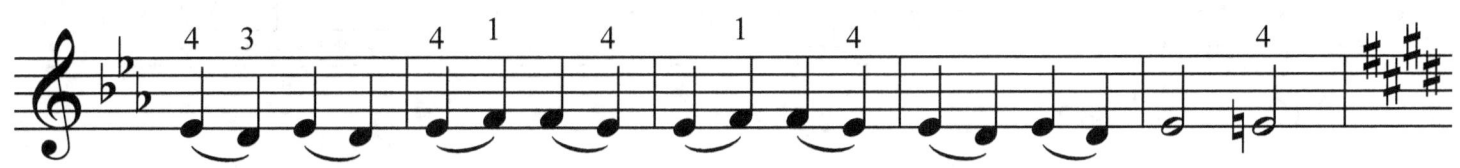

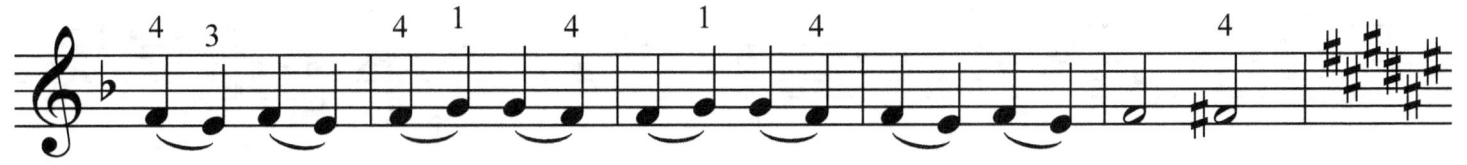

©2011 C. Harvey Publications All Rights Reserved.

2

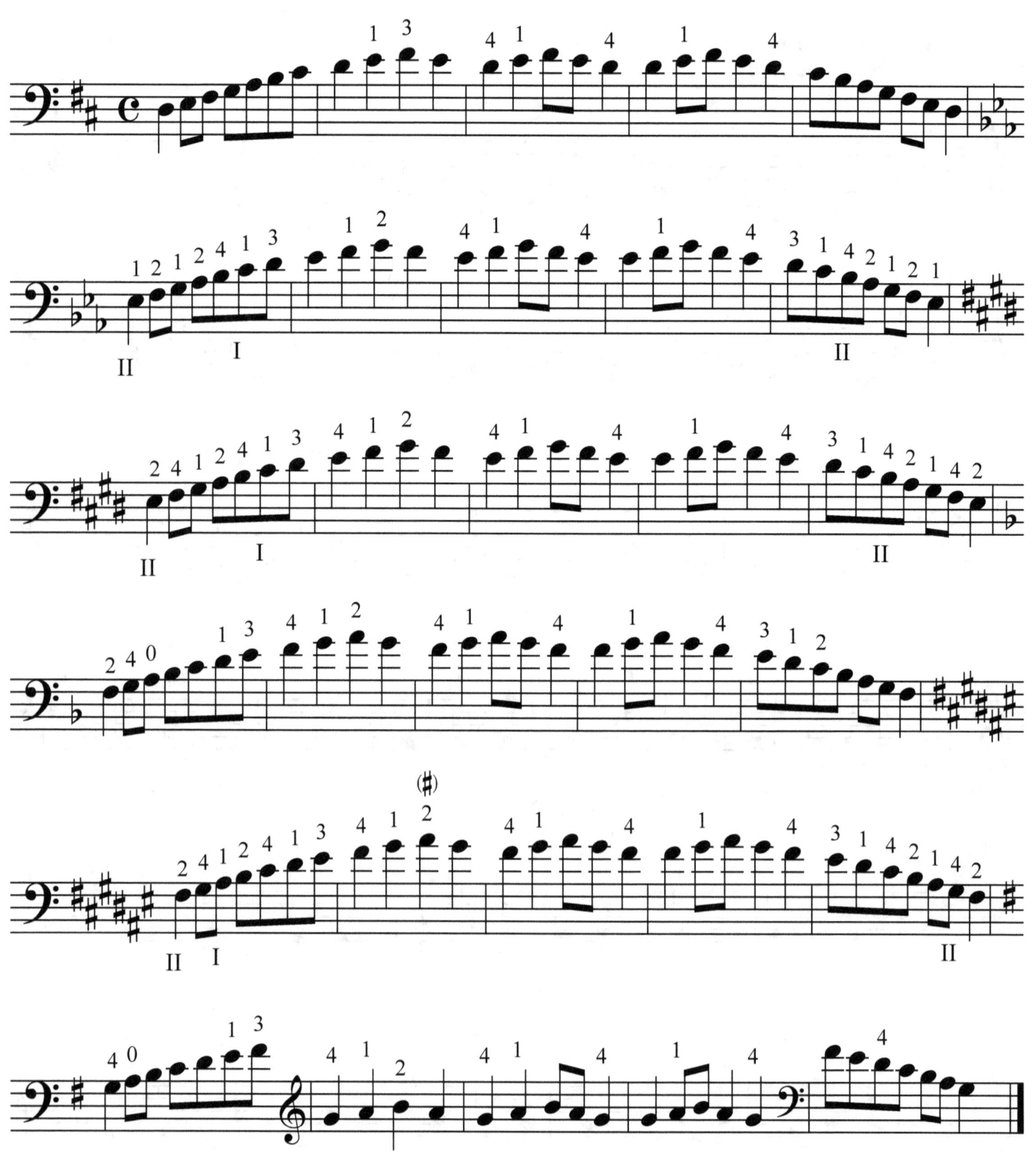

3

4

half step

5

6

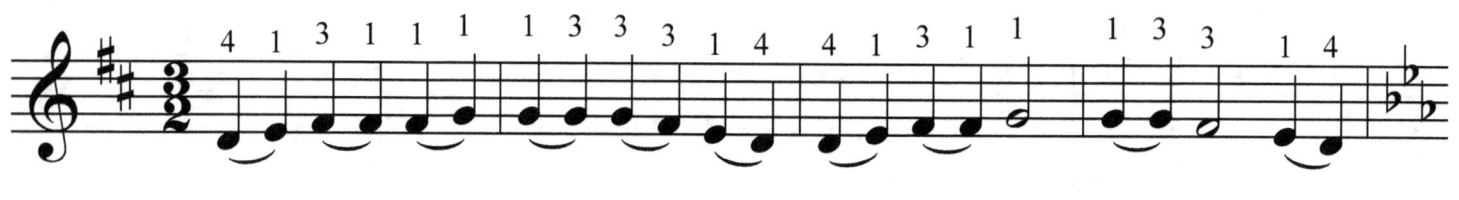
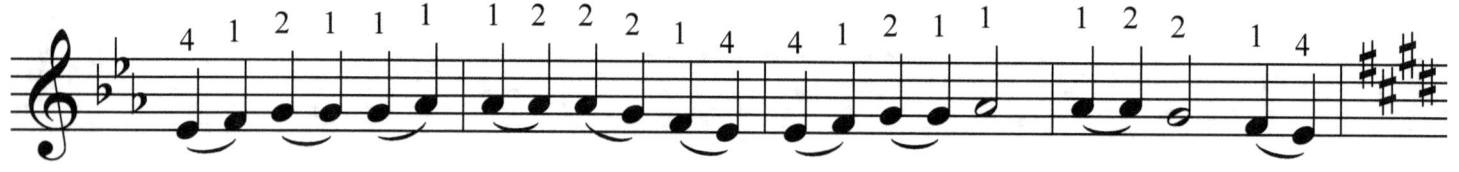

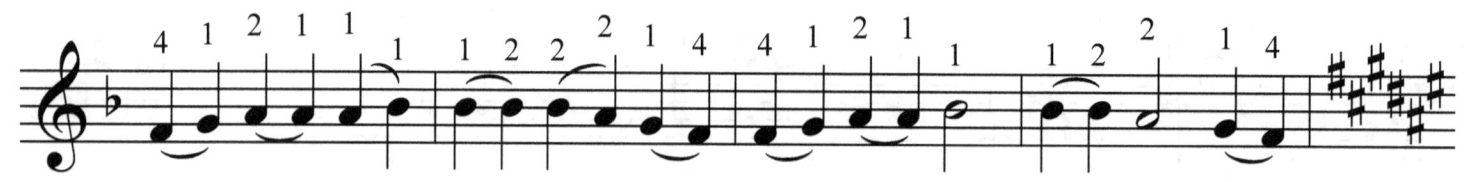

Scale Studies for the Third Octave, for the Cello, Book One

7

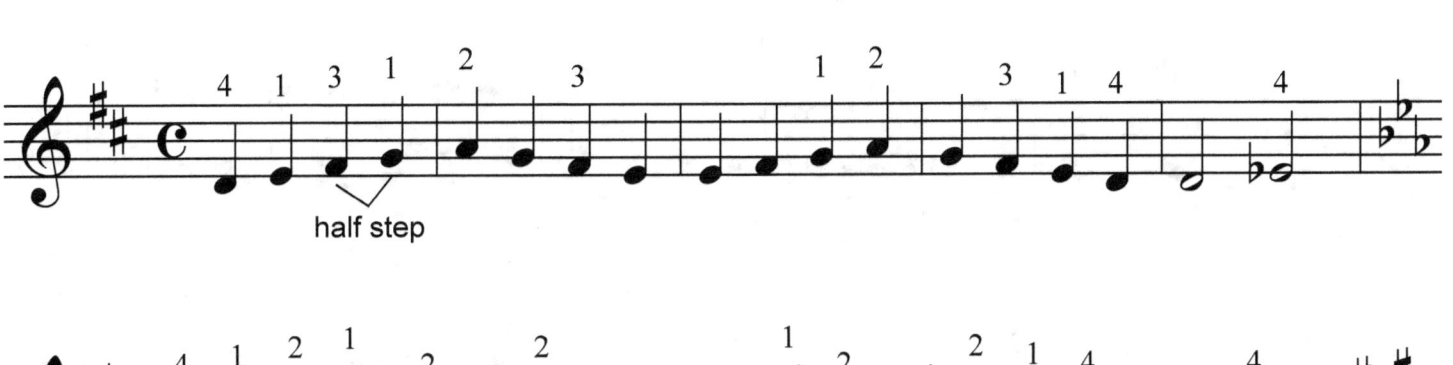
half step

©2011 C. Harvey Publications All Rights Reserved.

8

9

10

half step

Scale Studies for the Third Octave, for the Cello, Book One

11

©2011 C. Harvey Publications All Rights Reserved.

12

Scale Studies for the Third Octave, for the Cello, Book One

13

©2011 C. Harvey Publications All Rights Reserved.

14

15

16

17

18

Scale Studies for the Third Octave, for the Cello, Book One

19

©2011 C. Harvey Publications All Rights Reserved.

20

Scale Studies for the Third Octave, for the Cello, Book One

If you have difficulty finding the starting note
for exercises 21-29, play this first:

©2011 C. Harvey Publications All Rights Reserved.

22

23

24

25

26

©2011 C. Harvey Publications All Rights Reserved.

27

28

29

30

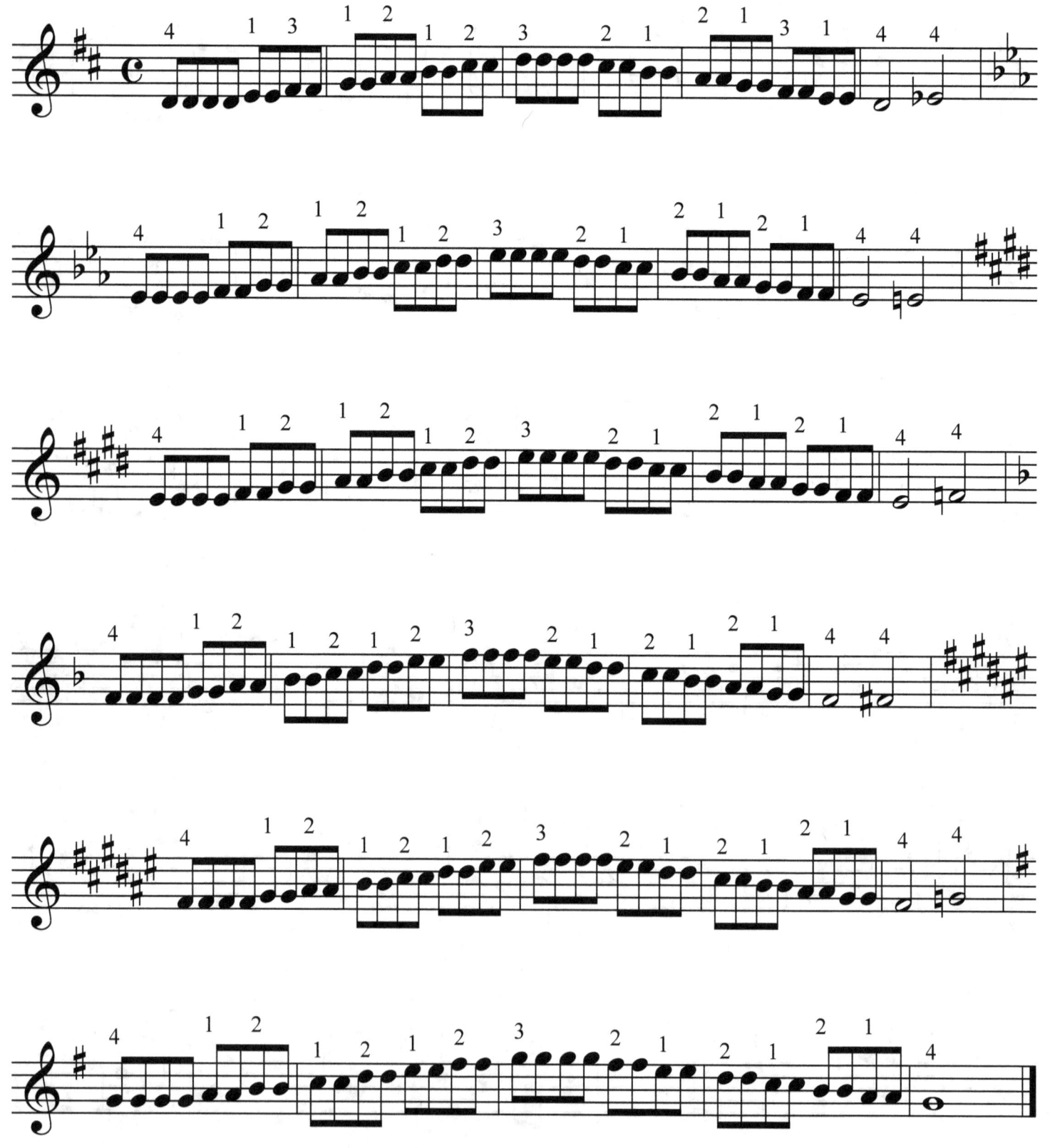

Scale Studies for the Third Octave, for the Cello, Book One

31

©2011 C. Harvey Publications All Rights Reserved.

32

33

34

Scale Studies for the Third Octave, for the Cello, Book One

35

©2011 C. Harvey Publications All Rights Reserved.

36

37

Staccato; on the string

38

Scale Studies for the Third Octave, for the Cello, Book One

39

©2011 C. Harvey Publications All Rights Reserved.

40

Scale Studies for the Third Octave, for the Cello, Book One

41

©2011 C. Harvey Publications All Rights Reserved.

42

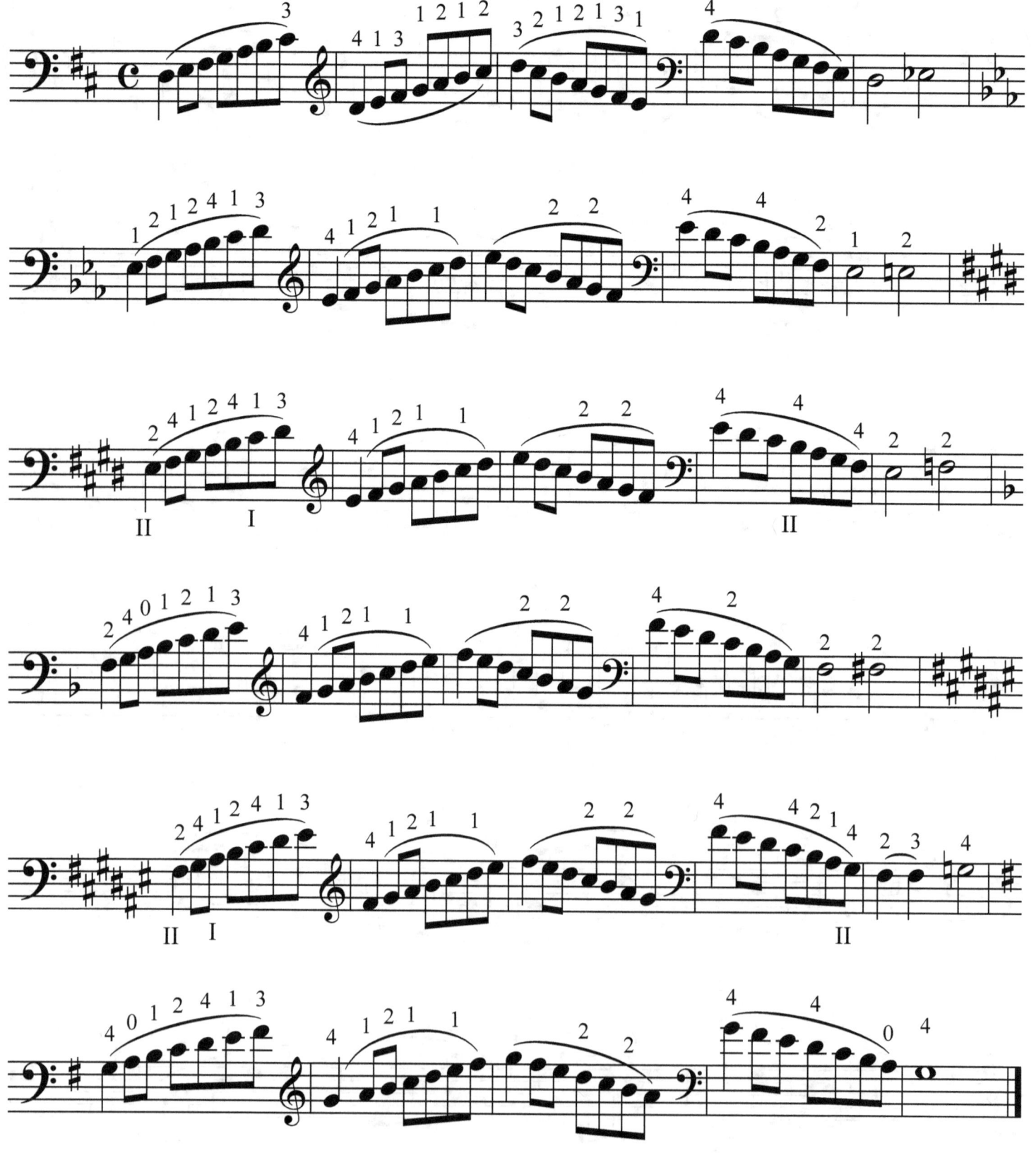

Scale Studies for the Third Octave, for the Cello, Book One

D major (sharps: F and C)

E-flat major (flats: B, E, and A)

E major (sharps: F, C, G, and D)

©2011 C. Harvey Publications All Rights Reserved.

F major (flat: B)

F-sharp major (sharps F, C, G, D, A, and E)

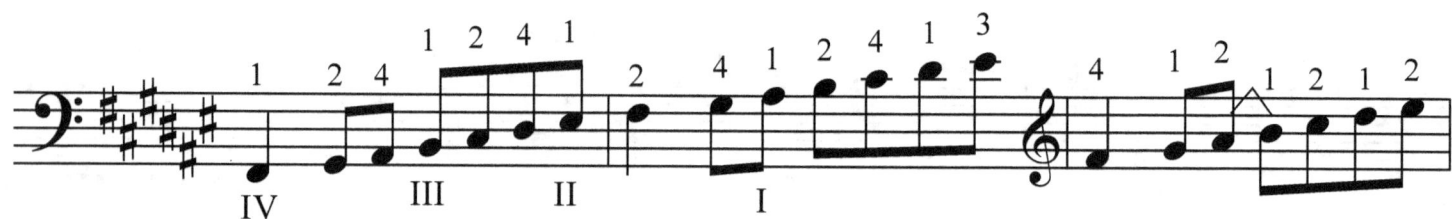

G major (sharp: F)

©2011 C. Harvey Publications All Rights Reserved.

also available from www.charveypublications.com
CHP210

Scale Studies for the Third Octave, for the Cello

1

Book Two
Cassia Harvey

Note: The scales studied in this book are listed at the end.

©2012 C. Harvey Publications All Rights Reserved.